MW01592906

A Walk in God's Garden

Poetic Expression

Written by Evelyn Chapman Daniel

Patricia Komen
for Evelyn Chapman Daniel

Dedication

I dedicated this book to the memory of my late husband, Raymond, and our oldest son, Rick, who during their lives, had always given me encouragement and inspiration in my writings.

Special Dedication

A special dedication goes to my daughters, Judith and Patricia, and to my son, Timothy. Their love, their support, their help and their lives have always encouraged, and inspired me in my written expressions. My family has always been upper most in the inspiration of my writings.

Evelyn Chapman Daniel

February 25, 1933 to February 15, 2002

A little note about my mother, Evelyn.

Mom, as we, my sisters and brothers called her, was a composer of songs, a writer of short stories and a writer of poetry. She called these her "writings". Her songs were sung in churches and her words spoken to audiences across Colorado. She created, designed and taught her program entitled "Poetic Expression" and served as a Poet-In-Residence in schools and lectured at the American Orff Schulwerk Association Rocky Mountain Chapter of Music Teachers. She continued sharing her gift with the Denver Academy of Music Summer Program, "Music, Dance & Poetry", Conferences for the Colorado Department of Education and the Graduate Study Program at Colorado University.

Memories surfaced in a corner of my mind as I began the work of readying Mom's writings for publishing. I recall she always had a pen or pencil in hand or within reach and wrote on envelopes, scraps of paper - anything that would receive her writings. She compiled these works of art to be published. However, life took her, as it does, on another journey where her health diminished and God found her waiting. Her writings lay wanting eventually making their way to my home where I tried as best I could to order them as she would want. Some I could not find so I will look and maybe add them another time. There are so many more. Perhaps another book of Evelyn Chapman Daniel's writings. -- Patricia Daniel Komar

Forward

Poetry and Poetic Expression can often, in all its brevity, express more feelings and emotions than the long written word of prose. An awakening of thoughts, an action of appliance, a strengthening of self-awareness can all be expressed every vividly. The writings in this book are all expressive and meaningful; some might make you smile, some might make you cry, others might make you wonder and you will learn from them. Some might make you see things in ways that you have never seen them before. Many moods and many emotions are expressed in various levels through the intermingling of thought and imagination.

The collection of writings in this book have been put together for you, the reader, that you might see, share, and enjoy as you walk along the path in "God's Garden."

Written by Evelyn Chapman Daniel

Table of Contents

Always a Star

Love Will Always Abound

The Harvest

To You, My Mother

Love Forever

Recipe for a Lasting Love

To Love

Wedded Bliss

I'm Going to Have a Baby

A Mother's Loving Thoughts

A Man

Our Son

Shadows of Darkness

Retreat to the Past

The Brighter Day

The Search

My Father, My Dad

Memories

I'm Just Resting

God's Love

If

Dreams

Go Forward

Credimus

Come Walk with Me

Author's note

There are many steps to be taken in a walk in God's garden. Not only the steps in seeing the natural beauty in the world around us, but also hearing the sounds, the singing of the birds, the swishing of the leaves on the trees. There are also the feelings, the warmth of the air, the briskness of the winds blowing around or body. All the aspects of life --- the sights, sounds, and feelings that touch our physical senses.

A walk in God's garden can also make one aware of the feelings which can affect our journey --- the joys, the love, the brightness of the days. Dark shadows may also be encountered ---- tragedies, illness, sadness and sorrows, however, through our faith, we will find that God is always with us, an arm on our shoulder guiding the way.

Moments of Solitude

I love the early morning hours
Before the break of down
When all is quiet and the world is still
Before the day moves on.
Within those quiet, early moments
I take the time to know
Moments of deep reflection
When my thoughts can quietly grow.
I reflect upon my blessings
Passed over through the day
And brought to light in Thanksgiving
With words of prayers I say
"Oh Lord, I thank thee for thy blessings
For the world of Nature around,
For every little song of bird,
Every growth from the earthly ground.
"For every limb that grows from a tree
Every leaf that blows
Every weed with beauty in sight
Every flake of falling snow.
"I thank thee for the sights and sound

The feelings in the air,
I thank thee for these moments
When I know, your presence is there."

My Church

The wide world around me is
My Church,
The sky above is its steeple,
All Nature's growth are its symbols,
The congregation --- all people.
People of colors, and all foreign lands,
Of mixed nations and breed,
Of different thoughts but only one God
All languages, all races and creed.
Yes – the world around me is
My Church,
The sky above is its steeple,
All Nature's growth are its symbols,
The congregation --- all people.
Only one God

All God's Children

From across the shores
of the ocean wide

And the waters from the distant sea,

From beyond the land of the
high horizon

The deserts, the hills, and prairie,

We come from all nations,
all languages and faith,

There is no color that
sets us apart

For our love is from our God

A love held deep in our heart.

We hear the voice of His Children
and the stories we have been told,

We know the voice of our inner souls
and the warmth of the Hand we hold.

For we are the children of our God
no color sets us apart,

We all walk together
in the world we trod

Our hands are all touched
by the strength of our God.

Beneath the Hands of God

Sometimes we must take a walk
along a shaded road

And when we tire --- must sit and rest
laying down a burdensome load.

We must listen to the whispers
of the echoes of the past

And view the distant shadows
and the role where we are cast.

We must look upon the open path
which we are about to trod

And lay the future forward
beneath the

Hands of God.

Prayers of Asking

I looked to the east at sunrise
before the day had begun,

And in my prayers, I requested
to be guided with the sun.

I asked for infinite wisdom
to follow a path which lay,

I asked for the helpful guidance
in the words I write and say.

And in my prayers of asking

I wonder if God could hear,

And I heard the song of a sparrow
echo in my ear.

I felt the warmth of God's presence
in the sounds of the world nearby.

I looked again to the sunrise ----
the sun was now bright in the sky.

The Silent Sounds

Silent sounds
of the evening
continue through
the night.

Quiet sounds,
whishing,
whispering,

Echoes of the moments

Echoes through the hours
of the day,

Through the evening
and the hours of the night.

Silent echoes through
the early morn.

Quiet sounds,

Silent sounds

And the stillness then
moves on.

The Walk

I walk along the hillside
and look to the setting sun

With quiet thoughts in solitude
as the light of the day is done.

My heart is troubled with worry
longing for a voice to hear,

And a message comes so softly
reflecting upon my ear.

"Just turn your troubles to me, oh child,

I'll help you along the way
to face again the morrow
and guide you through the day.

"I'll hold your hand in comfort,
strength will soon to come,

Ne'er to feel in solitude
for we both shall walk as one."

The Seasonal Voice of Life

****

The sound of the earth relinquishes
echoes of growing silence.

Soft patterns of rhythmic beats
quiet the stillness of soft breezes
blowing against my restless soul.

A tranquilizing voice of Life.

Oh, For a Moment

Oh, for a moment
When the air is still,
When the peace of tranquility
Drifts over the hill.
When the drone of quiet swallows
Flutters through the air,
And the voice of quiet echoes
Leaves without a care.

Countryside Expressions

There is such a peace in the countryside
That quiets the longing soul
Blending the stillness of the earth
With the beat of Nature's role.
Where the greenness of the meadows
And the wide expanse of sky
Embrace the arms of beauty
As quiet breezes sigh.
The sunrise in the morning
And the ground so fresh with dew
And the sunset in the evening
Give forth a call for you.
For I long to share this beauty,
The freshness of the Heavens above,
And let you feel that abundant warmth
The expression of God's Holy Love.

Peaceful River Valley

In the peaceful river valley
Where the wind blows quiet and still
The sound of Nature's footsteps
Gently ascend the distant hill.
Where the call of life is tending
Where the hand of God resounds
Where the touch of beauty tingles
The soul of the earth rebounds,
There lies the heart of being
Where veins of root run strong
As the beat of a whisper, trend of a cell
Symbolic melody of psalm.

Yesterday's Pines

One path was there leading 'round the bend
Barely downtrodden -- and yet no end
Onward and upward ascending the hill
Footprints of the past -- showing still.
An old tin can -- rusty with age
An abandoned cabin -- history's page
A fallen log -- old with decay
Sign of old -- another day.
Around the bend -- upward and on
New days, new nights, the breaking dawn
The future rolls past -- tomorrows signs
The fallen needles of yesterday's pines.

The Seasons' Beauty

From the frosted white snow of the winter
to the budding blossoms of spring,
the warm, blue skies of summer
and the colors autumn will bring,

The seasons show their beauty
on the earth on which we trod,
touched by the artist's paint brush
lovingly held in the hands of our God.

And, oh, the beauty of seasons
when the earth bursts forth in bloom,
and the warmth of love around us
all come from God's Holy Room.

Oh, Lilac Bud

Oh, lilac bud upon the bush
It is only January -- what is the rush?
Winter is not gone -- the snow is still here,
If you bud too early -- you'll freeze, I fear.
The warmth of spring will be here soon
And kiss your stems -- then you can bloom,
Hide away now, lilac bud, hide away beep,
You can come out when winters asleep.

The Lonesome Bud

There was a rose that did not open
yet lasted throughout the cold,

When it was found in the spring of the year
her petals were dried and cold.

Perfection of the lonesome bud
was majestic and mystic to see,

Outliving the long, harsh winter,
a delicate, but regal beauty.

Her stems were dried from the bitter cold,
her leaves were burned from the frost.

Yet still the staunch was lifting high,

Her lasting beauty was not lost.

The new growth of spring was fresh at the base,

The living --- the rebirth that grows,

Energy flowing from the old to the new ---

Reborn --- the Beauty of the Rose.

A Peekin' Up at Me

Guess what I just saw a peekin'
up at me?

So daring, unwitting, enticingly,

Yes --- enticing it was --- just
poppin' thru,

I wanted to join it and start
poppin' too.

Delicate as a jewel, so shiny and clean,

I filled with delight as I knew I had seen

The fresh beginning that newness
can bring,

The new stem of growth,

The first sign of spring.

That Special Garden

That special garden some can't see

The joy and beauty the weeds bring to me.

They may call them pests, they cut and
they plow,

That rake and they burn, they hate
them to grow.

But I look and I smile for I know
they'll return,

Gold plants and God waters, someday
they'll learn.

Raking and cultivating and the seeds
will grow

I don't have to worry, you see,
I know.

In the garden of flowers, the vegetable rows,

The yards and playgrounds, the rains and the snows,

The pathways and roadsides, the fields and hills

I know it they die .... they'll grow there still.

God does the planting of the seeds
giving then such loving care,

Returning each year, those beautiful weeds,

*My special garden
will always be there.*

This is Mine

When I see the summer swallows
Spread their wings and fly
I sense the peace of the country
As they gracefully glide thru the sky.
Thru the open sky of the country
Thru the sunset of summer time
Thru open trails of gentle breezes
And they whisper, "This is mine".
And oh, they love their freedom
Where they can bend, and spread their wings
Where the sound of their voices can echo
With the tone that nature brings.

Waves of Nature

Beneath the sprawling cottonwood tree
Thick branches and leaves give shade to me
Soft, cool breezes briskly blowing,
Peaceful solitude gently flowing.
Red-wing Blackbirds fluttering of wings,
Warbling canaries busily sing.
Chipmunks and squirrels stealthily play
The waves of Nature give forth the day.

Silhouette

The peaceful mood of autumn
(Though it seems a summer still)
Reflects the flame of sunset
Beyond the distant hill.
Where tranquil shadows of twilight
'Midst echoes of the day
Resound the call of nature
As the silhouette, will lay.
Among the lasting beauty
of dark against light
Artistic strokes of brushwork
As day returns into night.
The twilight shadows of autumn
Now greet the winter's song
The warmth of summer's sunshine
Though silently lingers on.

The Autumn Day

I look upon the colors

And wonder from whence they come

Have they come from the touch of Nature?

Have they come from the touch of the sun?

And why the reds and the yellows

And why the orange and browns?

And why has the green of summer

Turned into an earthly crown?

Is there magic that's hidden in secret

Giving forth a mystical ray

Bringing his colorful beauty

And calling it "The Autumn Day?"

Harvest of Seasons

Within the midst of autumn
when leaves begin to fall,

Redolent passage of nature
gives forth a seasonal call.

Where embers of flame and fire
and mists of amber gold

And rusts of burnish umber---

The promise of futures is told.

It is in the future of winter
when earth prepares for spring

Seeds burst forth and blossom
and the white snow turns green.

The warmth of summer sunlight
turns the sky a deepened blue,

Leaves and blossoms flourish
in the greenish summer hue.

But in the midst of autumn
rewards of nature are sent

In the flaming glory of colors
as the "Harvest of Seasons" is spent.

Seasonal Wonders

Wither Wonderland, silver and gold,

Autumn and winter, seasonal cold,

Leaves still falling, flakes of snow,

Early snowfall, diamonds bright glow.

Footprints tracing a path through the snow

Where they lead to, I do not know.

Perhaps it be to an early spring,

Seasonal wonder, wondrous thing.

The Winter Chill

I wandered through the silver brush
Crystal ice and snow,
Aimlessly, relentlessly, not knowing
where to go.
The ground was hard with the winter's chill
I pushed stiff branches away,
Frozen with snow, falling and cold,
Extending my arms, I opened the way.
The world before me glittered
As of metal, iron and steel,
The shining cast of aluminum
Somehow seemed not real.
Never in my wandering
Had I seen the world so white,
Where the darkened core of blackness
Removed away with the snow of night.

Peaceful Beauty

In the realm of peaceful beauty
Rest the mountains mighty tall,
In the stream of rippling waters
Lay the flow of Nature's call.
In the glow of the garden sunset
Mount clouds of lasting peace
Blowing the breeze of twilight ending
For the light of day shall cease.
As the twilight shadows appear
And the sun sets down in the west
Echoes are quiet in the evening sky
And day is now laid to rest.

Always a Star

There is always a star

Shining brightly

To guide you on your way

Along the path to follow
in every future day.

Just look to the stars
in the Heavens

Shining forth the warmth
of God's love

Hold tight to the glittering
beauty

The stars shining brightly above.

The stars are there to guide you

On the path on which you trod

Shining brightly the fullest glory

Leading on to our Heavenly God

Love Will Always Abound

Authors Note

The journey through God's Garden also takes up along a path of "compassion." That is, the expression of Love --- the caring, the sharing, the advising, inspiring, prayers, concerns --- so many more. All feelings that God has instilled in us in the showing of everyday life --- words and expressions that come from the heart, for others.

I am also sharing with you, the reader, some of the finding and happenings in my life which have helped me be so aware of God's presence --- the strength and love touching my shoulders. There has always been a light that seemed to shine and brighten my way through the journey of Life.

As steps are taken in the journey through God's Garden, shadows and gray clouds may be encountered. It is difficult to understand sometimes, the mysteries of life and why they occur. However, our faith and the love of God helps us find our way.

Included in this segment of writings are a few of my poetic expressions written at times when I was emotionally trying to find my own way through the gray clouds.

The Harvest

A seed of thought in every home

A root from which to grow

A grain of wheat,

A mustard seed,

A plant to care and sow.

To nature, and to treasure,

To blossom forth its bloom,

To feed to the world
in wisdom

Grown forth from

God's Holy Room.

---- Evelyn Chapman Daniel

To You, My Mother

From the time that I was little
I could always turn to you
to help with little problems
and things I'd want to do.

I know that you would listen
to my problems, a great or small,
That you would make them all seem less
as if no problem at all.

You always make the world seem bright
with smiles and words of cheer
with guidance and wisdom
and a strong lasting love
into each day and passing year.

Mom, I Love You.

Your daughter,

Evelyn

Written by Evelyn Chapman Daniel

Love Forever

Before we met, I knew you
A love in my heart I shared,
Before we met I touched you
For in my dreams, I cared.
And in those moments of dreaming
I knew that it would be
The two of us together
Our lives, just you and me.
And when our paths we found had crossed
And our hands reached out for the other,
I knew that we had met before
And our love would be forever.

--- Evelyn Chapman Daniel

Recipe for a Lasting Love

Heat over an open fire ....

Two hearts full of:
Longing dreams   warm desire
fond affection   cherished devotion

Add:
several tender kisses
one warm passionate embrace
a touch of tingling excitement

Shake together vigorously and allow to blossom freely.

Rekindle fire as needed.

Service for two.

To Love

To love is to cherish
To covet, to hold,
Regard and respect
As pages of gold.
To have in one's dreams …
Nothing can mar,
To never let go …
No matter how far.
To hug and caress …
No harm to be done,
To love is your life
In sharing with one.

Wedded Bliss

There is many a special secret
That makes for wedded bliss,
The sharing, the caring,
Each tender touch, each loving kiss.
The love, the joy, the laughter,
The struggles, and yes, the tears,
Tribulations, and trials
Through each and every year.
Patience, consideration and tolerance
Through problems and through strife,
The sacrifice of "Giving"
Unselfish devotion of "life."
---Evelyn Chapman Daniel

I'm Going to Have a Baby

Oh, what a joy to be able to say
"I'm going to have a baby."
What a joy to be able to
Anticipate its birth.
To know the growth which
Is born in you
Will burst forth and bring its own love.
No object or living thing
Can compare with the love
A baby can bring.
It spreads its love on angel wings
Into the arms to hold,
Bringing joy and lasting pride
Embraced in blankets of gold.

A Mother's Loving Thoughts

Unselfish love I'll give to him,
abiding strength to hold,

A babe in arms he is just now
mine to covet, gracefully mold.

And through his days and months
and years

I'll give him courage to fight his fears.

I'll hear him laugh, I'll hear him cry,

Perhaps a little, too, will I.

A babe in arms he is just now,

Closely held to my breast,

Soft in my arms so tenderly,

Someday he'll leave the nest.

Until that time, too soon to come,

I must prepare my baby son
to be the man must be

The day he'll wave good-by to me.

-- Evelyn Chapman Daniel

A Man

A Man is a man who can give off himself
And not bury himself in his soul,
A man is a man who will bravely stand
When fear threatens to take its toll.
A Man is a man who can be a friend
To the friendless and those in need,
Reaching his arm and giving a hand
In performing a kindly deed.
A Man is a man who makes use of the gifts
Which God has bestowed in his care,
A Man is a man who helps others to grow –
His knowledge, his talents he'll share
A Man is a man who will yield not
To temptations to prove his might,
His conscience will lead him,
His conscience will guide him,
And show him the way of the right.
A Man is a man who looks for a challenge –
Its success he will strive to gain,
If he should stumble, if he should fall –
He will rise and try again.

A Man is measured by the goodness he does,

How fully he lives his life,

The strength he shows when strength is needed

In the face of problems and strife.

Any or all of these attributes

Is a challenge for a man to test.

If in failing, he sincerely can say,

"I tried, I tried to do my best"

This too, then, is a Man.

Our Son

A babe in arms
we cuddled him,

A boy ---
we watched him grow.

A man of youth
he went his way,

And we were proud.

We gave him guidance,

We gave him love,

We gave him strength
to hold.

And in a moment
of joy conceived –

In return
we, too, received.

A thankful note

O, God, we pray
that for a time
he came our way.

Shadows of Darkness

I looked to the skies in the Heavens

--- No sun was shining there,

I looked to the trees blooming gently

--- Feeling not warmth of air.

I walked through the garden of flowers
budding no blossom of bloom.

Feeling the darkness of agony
and foreboding blanket of gloom.

Where is God's hand of guidance?

Where are the arms to hold?

Where is the warmth of brightness
to rid the days of cold?

The rains are falling lightly,
grey fog begins to grow,

The mist of shadows descending
as winds begin to blow.

"Oh, lead her to the comfort
where lights are warm and bright,

Lead forth to protective shelter
of a painless, peaceful night.

Retreat to the Past

One path was there
downtrodden and bare,

History's page remaining there.

Moving downward in quick descent

No time for thought nor lengthy repent.

Tracing the footprints, those fallen before

Failures of history -- who closed the door.

The easy beginning -- the struggles not last

The easy way down -- retreat to the past.

Which path is yours -- which do you take?

Do not be hasty in the choice you make.

Give thoughtful care, it's a difficult task,

Do you move to the future
or
Retreat to the past

The Brighter Day

It is hard sometimes to understand
why things happen to like they do.

We wonder where we'll get the strength
to always see them through.

But it doesn't hurt to wonder
and ask our questions of "Why"

Often times the answers may only
be found in the Heavenly sky.

Wondering and searching for answers

Much strength can then be found

Through Faith, through family,
through friendships. . . . . . .
abundantly around.

We search for understanding
and guidance along the way,

And through our Faith

God shows us

There will be a Brighter Day.

The Search

I looked one day for the sunshine
Searching through clouds of gray
Finding but darkened shadows
That seemed to drift our way.
Then one day the sun appeared
As in answer to a prayer
Shining bright its fullest glory
As if it had always been there.
And oh, the glory of sunshine
When you search and then you find
That sunshine is the faith in prayer
And the outlook in your mind.

My Father, My Dad

With wisdom of guidance
he holds my hand
Helping me always
to understand.

Giving me laughter
to chase my tears
Strength and comfort
to hide my fears.

The years have been special
the good and the bad.
He walks with me always
My father,
My Dad.

Memories

Memories are the treasures....
Each thought, word, and deed,
Each tender touch, each loving kiss,
Special moments of quiet bliss.
The joys and the laughter,
The sorrows and the tears,
Unselfish moments giving
Through each and every year.
Yes, memories are the treasures
Moments never to part,
Embraced with warmth and tenderness
Always held close to the heart.

I'm Just Resting

I seem to go in circles
The trails in my mind.
It seems the years are beginning to show
My age ------ I'm not resigned.
I seem to sit and reminisce
And watch the time pass by
And then my eyes will open wide
And I wonder how it can fly.

I can't keep up with what's going on
My legs don't move as fast.
They seem to be dragging --- my footsteps have slowed
And the world is moving right past.
But then there's times I look around
And watch the generations anew
And wonder how many can catch up with me
And keep up with what I do.

So maybe I deserve the rest
Though sure as it may be
To just lay back and look around
And see what I can see.

And though I know I'll not retire
But just resting for a while
I'll just relax and close my eyes
And I'll wake up with a smile.

God's Love

I felt the warmth of a loving hand
and heard the silent prayer,

I felt the strength of life renewed
and knew my life was there.

"Oh, Mom, Oh, Mom

You've made it through,

Oh, Mom, Oh, Mom

How we do love you."

The strength of love was all around,

Tears fell from their eyes,

My family, my minister, my friends,

All were speaking their loving cries.

All were witness to the strength of Life,

All were witness to the God's Holy Love,

All were witness to the miracle healing

All had come from the Heaven's above.

Lord, I thank you.

If

If I could bring a bit of joy
To someone's unhappy heart
Or show at least I understand
When they and their loved ones part,
If I could be a friendly companion
To those who have lonesome hours
And share my faith with those who wonder
Who or what has higher powers,
If I could bring a big of laughter
To those who don't know how
I'd not put it off another minute-----
I'd do it all right now.

Dreams

There is always a dream worth dreaming
Always a wish come true,
Always a star in the future
Waiting just for you.
Let moments of the past be forgotten,
Let dreams of the future hold true.
Dreams of the days' forthcoming
Will bring solace and happiness to you.
Dreams are the hands of the future,
And the hands are the warmth of each day.
Days are the molds forthcoming
Where strength of happiness will lay.

Go Forward

There is always a star
That is beckoning.
Always a mountain to climb
Always a pathway to follow
Always a hand to guide
Always a voice that will whisper. ...
"Come, be on your way,
Into the future, go forward,
Live to the fullest each day."
            ---Evelyn Chapman Daniel

Credimus

Make the most of each day as it comes

Let each breath relinquish a prayer

Let each word that is spoken

Each thought, deed of token

Be worth of the life that is there.

Let the path of footsteps be guided

Let the hands of souls far and neat

Be led by the strength and power

The touch and faith we hold dear.

Let the moments of life everlasting

Be held with regard, us too late

And the trialed and joys of a life time

Be of duties, and service and fate.

Let the trust of the mind be guided

In the length of the world we trod

By belief and the truth of a power

In the strength in the hands of our God.

Let the trials of the past be forgotten

Let the dream of the dreams of the future hold true

And reward of the Heavens be give

In the light that will shine upon you. ----EC. Daniel